DAVID McPHAIL'S
ANIMALS A to Z

DAVID McPHAIL'S
ANIMALS A to Z

SCHOLASTIC INC. / *New York*

SCHOLASTIC
HARDCOVER

Library of Congress Cataloging-in-Publication Data
McPhail, David
Animals A to Z.
Summary: The reader may search pictures to find
animals whose names begin with each letter of the
alphabet.
1. English language—Alphabet—Juvenile literature.
2. Animals—Juvenile literature. [1. Animals—Pictorial
works. 2. Alphabet] I. McPhail, David, ill. II. Title.
PE1155.M28 1988 [E]   87-4955
ISBN 0-590-40715-5

12 11 10 9 8 7 6 5 4 3 2 1   8 9/8 0 1 2 3/9

Printed in U.S.A.   23

FIRST SCHOLASTIC PRINTING, FEBRUARY 1988

A

B

C

E

F

G

H

K

M

N

P

R

S

T

U

Y

Armadillo

Bear, Bird

Cricket, Crocodile, Crow

Dog, Duck

Eel, Egret, Elephant

Fish, Fox, Frog

Goose, Gorilla

Hedgehog, Horse

Iguana

Jaguar

Kangaroos

Ladybug, Lion

Moose, Mouse

Nightingale

Owl

Porcupine

Quail

Rabbit, Rhinoceros, Robin

Swan

Tiger, Turtle

Unicorn, Upside-down catfish

Vulture

Walrus, Whale, Wolf

Xenops

Yak

Zebra

McPhail, David M.
   David McPhail's animals A to Z. --
New York : Scholastic Inc., c1988.
   [26] p. : col. ill. ; 21 cm.

   Summary: The artist's illustrations
present a painting of at least one
animal for each letter of the alphabet.

   ISBN 0-590-40715-5

   1. Alphabet--Juvenile literature. 2.
Animals--Juvenile literature. 3.
Concepts--Juvenile literature. I.
Title II. Title: Animals A to Z.